BRINE ORCHID

ARAH KO

BRINE ORCHID

POEMS

YESYES BOOKS

Brine Orchid © 2025 by Arah Ko

NO AI TRAINING: Without in any way limiting the author's exclusive rights under copyright, any use of this publication to "train" generative artificial intelligence (AI) technologies to generate text is expressly prohibited. The author reserves all rights to license uses of this work for generative AI training and development of machine learning language models.

Cover and Interior Design: Olivia M. Hammerman
Project Lead: Gale Marie Thompson
Author Photograph: Marcus Jackson

ISBN: 978-1-946303-10-3
Printed in the United States of America

Published by YesYes Books
Portland, Oregon
YesYesBooks.com

KMA Sullivan, Publisher
Karah Kemmerly, Managing Editor
Gale Marie Thompson, Senior Editor
Jill Kolongowski, Manuscript Copy Editor
James Sullivan, Assistant Editor

For my family

"I said to the sun / tell me about the Big Bang / The sun said, 'It hurts to become.'"
—Andrea Gibson

CONTENTS

Origin Myth *1*
Phantom Pain As Natal Philopatry *5*
Sinter *6*
Her Name Was Daphne *8*
Out of the Eater *9*
Kumiho 구미호 *11*
Astraphobia *13*
Glister *14*
My Body Is the Ancestor I Never Knew *15*
My Father after Korea *17*
Second Tongue *18*
Telephobia *19*
As If It Never Happened *20*
God of Dew *21*
Legend *22*
Mouthful of Orchids *24*
Cullet *25*
Haole Girl *26*
Dol 돌 *27*
Galatea Again *29*
Cruel Instincts *30*
A Star Is Collapsing in Cygnus *31*
First Hymn *32*
Thalassophobia *33*
Burning the Ships *34*
Glass Eel *35*
Fish Eye *36*
Gretel & Hansel When Asked Why They Are Hungry *41*

My Grandmother after Korea *42*
Latching *43*
The Wolf, Remembered *44*
Vampire Plants Talk to Their Victims While Drinking *45*
Turtle Ship *47*
Danji Girl *49*
Phaedra *50*
Light a Candle *51*
Claustrophobia *52*
I Want to Want to Get Better *53*
Epistle of Eve *54*
Haole Sonnet *55*
The Milky Way Dreams of the Big Bang *56*
DNA Test *57*
Backwards *58*
Fireline *60*
Origin of Species *62*
Ophidiophobia *65*
Lucid Fever *66*
Portrait of the Frightened in Recovery *67*
God's Love Is Very Loud *68*
Citrus Paradisi *69*
In Hawaiian, Haole Means Breathless *70*
The Poet's Guide to Translation *71*
Catching *72*
Ya'aburnee *74*
Miracle *76*
Lazarus *77*
Omphalophobia *78*
Origin of the Fear *80*
Notes *83*
Acknowledgments *87*

ORIGIN MYTH

Except it's not a myth: once I wasn't here and now
I am. We are. The cold shook-fist universe

                    dispersed stardust, gaseous breaths, gigantic cradle
                born bruised. Ripped space bleeding sun had nothing

in common with my squished, six-pound body shivering
upon my mother's bloody chest and father's

                    unbroken hand. I have decided to be happy
                    in spite of everything that came before

and because of it. I close my eyes and my grandmother
buries the unborn beneath a rose bush. Her mother

                    trembles down the aisle at fourteen. Meanwhile, great
                great grandmother tears floorboards out at the end of her life,

wanting to *feel the earth under my feet again.* Some blood
-lines are more sacred than dynasties. Outside

                    our time, my ancestor motions a prince with a sword,
                  black silk 한복 rasping against the blade. Steel

ripples like a mirror. The poet Adonis asks, *how
many centuries deep is your wound?* All I can answer is:

                    deep. Where is the beginning? My hands grope
                  through darkness for the damage. Somewhere, super

-novae debris congeals, solar lesions fold
into stellar embryos, my fingers still searching

                                       for rupture, umbilical cord, origin point. There are
                                           fledgling stars in this void, you and I in this

nebula. I'm not afraid anymore.

PHANTOM PAIN AS NATAL PHILOPATRY

There were no guns, but when the club
in the soldier's hand connected to the soft

skull in market square, you knew:
it was time to leave. Four lonely

decades later and you are still searching
for what you left in Korea: buried jar

of kimchi, silk hanbok, your Halabeoji's
grave. You gave up a hundred family

ghosts to transplant here. Now
the second generation spends

graduate school studying our roots
like an amputee reaching for lost limbs.

Sea turtles remember the beach where
they were born by smell, instinct, the pull

of the tide, but I was never good
at directions. Tell me: which parts am I missing?

SINTER

I didn't know
I was angry until lightning

pulverized the stream and I felt
nothing.

No quiver at the flashbulb
-struck riverbed

water leapt away from
like a cutdown dress.

No trembling
fear at static vapor

only a field from my tiny tin
can car humming

along a Midwest road.
Instead, I became brittle,

teeth ground down the way
they do at night,

jaw working away bone—
molars locked.

Under heat and pressure, some
substances and people

melt, soft warmth
giving up form

as molten glass, liquid gold. Others
sinter when struck—

brittle pieces break
off: iron, cullet, bone, sea

shell. Did you know parts
of you could splinter like hit flint,

shatter like volcanic glass?
If not,

you will.

I didn't stop to check
the flash termination,

smoldering entry
wound. I didn't

even look.

HER NAME WAS DAPHNE

While
I wait for you,

river rocks replace my teeth,
spiders, my hands;

pine needles brush my
naked shoulders.

I sleep slow winters
      in the forest, dream

of muddy smiles, long
      fingers tracing

the scars bears carved in
fall. Creatures pity;

squirrels sleep inside
      my breast, bees

lace my brain. Rain licks
      my body clean

with cold tears night
      after night,

like some sad god
has remembered me

and leaned down.

OUT OF THE EATER

I must find a way
out of this valley, its
donkey jaws, hyena
fur, the many glass
liquor bottles
impregnated with
liquid sun as they
undulate on my
windowsill like see
-through belly
dancers: they move
the way Delilah might
have, her fingers
tangled in so much
black hair. Her lover
always drunk
on rage & women
& hot honeycomb
clinging to the corpse
of the lion he tore
open with his own
bare hands. No one
survives this story.
My arm hairs rise
when I prod
my family tree for wine
-colored bruises: the
alcohol & violence,
my grandfather's
lush breath when he

beat his wife, broke
cups & doors, how
he stopped drinking
with a single prayer.
I pretend to know
how much strength
& uncut hair it takes
to outrun seven
generations of
fire. Is hope & wrath
within me, like the pit
in a peach?
Behind a lion's soft
black lips sleep
so many teeth.

KUMIHO 구미호

Little cub, baby fox, devious
one, have you eaten? My grandmother

brandishes garnished
banchan plates, decisive

as a general. *Our hands
are delicious*, she says, *everything*

we touch will taste so good. Her fingers
brush my lips, cup the apples

of my cheeks, thread through
my hair. Halabeoji laughs, his gray

mustache dancing on his upper lip.
Baby fox, he says, *you're growing*

tails, how clever you are! In legends,
each vixen tail is a measure

of cunning, centuries lived,
organs stolen. Who does not fear

the hungry spirit ghosting through
their walls, dressed as a bride,

her lethal yeowoo guseul swallowing
their life force? The deepest kiss:

a devouring. First, Halabeoji said I had
one, then three, now nine bushy

tails. *You look like me*, Halmeoni
laughs, old fox to young cub. Although

I wonder if I am fox enough,
sharp enough, my eyes not shaped

like hers. Halmuni bares
her teeth. What ravenous love

does she wish for me? *My darling child,*
she laughs, *oh mischievous one,*

how many hearts have you eaten?

ASTRAPHOBIA

Being struck by lightning must be
like being touched by God and not
knowing whether you will die. Hot
fission ripping through the air
plugs into bones and blood, fists
flexing, muscles crush with the seizing
heart. The odds of this are some
800 times less than being shot in my
area, dangers specific to this space
and era. In the dream I had
last night you were chosen as if
by a god, and nuzzled by the cold
nose of a gun, and I, not knowing
whether you would die, felt my mouth
open up to eject an endless vein of light,
electricity burning my throat on its way
out, fulgurous, inevitable. We call those
touched by lightning *lucky* because
we can't call it anything else.

GLISTER

Before the storm, all but one
window was boarded up. Beyond it,
palms writhed against vines, a green
-blooded chimera. A girl in a saffron dress
petalled on the floor, palms pressed to the one
window. Crystal sliver cold
as silk separated her skin from a torrent
of nocturnal rain. Shining cinch between her
and the wild, so soft and so sharp. Her mother,
in the other room, cold under silk. Her mother, a soap
bubble, pushing out the squall. The glazing warmed
against her hands. Her mother, warmed glass
against the darkness. The pane
a narrow glister in the night. The tempest
howled with a deadly kind of love.

MY BODY IS THE ANCESTOR I NEVER KNEW

They call me *progeniture cell.*
I move

in every direction. My edges brush
against the believable.

I wish someone had told me
my body is its own

instruction. Here, cilia wave
away the lethal,

there golden mitochondria
beam with indelible inner

light. My workings are
arcane. Inevitable, heady—

I, who am never more
drunk than anyone else,

dream each viable
future. A stem cell shimmers

with possibility, remembering
primordial shift, an ancient

sea, a whole, unbroken
bone. My every move

intoxicating in its exactness:

I can be anything that you want.
I can be everything that you need.

MY FATHER AFTER KOREA

All the stories you tell and this
is the part you skip over: the melted bridge,

a rash of marigolds blooming over
her shoulder, the way his body hit

the water: bones brittle as glass. Then
the press South, soldiers at the door:

그는 어디 있니? Halabeoji curled in the floor
boards, silent, or maybe it was after—his slack

mouth, soju bottles, thick knuckles folded
over pearls at the kitchen table. The sound

as the string snapped around your mother's
neck reminds you: it was never rewritten.

The white beads tinkle in your eomma's
drawstring bag all the way across the Pacific,

pouring your father, like silt, into liquor
bottles, one after another. The lingering stink

of Philadelphia, the city of brotherly
love where your younger brother vanished

in the same oily night which swallowed
the pearls, one by one.

SECOND TONGUE

Anyone can say they love you, but only my father will say *your face*

is like the moon. You might work, but he is bringing back the bacons. English

can be a slippery thing, a second tongue, a weapon. How many

times did it slice him? Stumbling off the greasy dock into the American

Dream. When men called him *yellow, slit-eyed, chink* and spat on the earth

his sneakers touched, he just laughed and said *my eyes only open a slither.*

My dad never complained about *hand me overs*, but when he requested

please, shit down with me, and the children laughed, he bit through his lip.

His grammar is impeccable. He painstakingly tutored me into a perfect

SAT score, declared, you can do it, you can have many slices of cakes

and pies and stuff and later, in my college years, I'm here if you need to get

something off your shoulder. Who can deny when the boat is gone, or that I am his

splitting image? You see, last week, when my father exclaimed, 아라야

how come your eyes are so loud? I understood him perfectly.

TELEPHOBIA

When you ask if I believe in *forever*,
demanding I decide, grasp the question

by its roots and pull, I remind you of my fear
of landlines. The insistent chiming, the way

my lungs transfigured into panicked doves,
wings beating my ribcage, how, as a child,

I hid from ringtone purring like a monster
and still leave you on read, let loved ones

dangle into voicemail. How can I explain
the void on the end of the line, anyone

could be calling? Deep space vibrates
like a low voice on a cell. Somewhere inside,

I want to destroy you, who I've loved enough
to write this poem, with tender words

some of which must survive, go on and on,
reverberating, the way that I love you, but not

enough. The way I think forever is not an answer,
but a question, a phone ringing.

AS IF IT NEVER HAPPENED

As if the collar never loosed around
my neck, the gold of Egypt offered

at my feet, the sea ripped, howling,
in half. As though the words were never

etched into the stone by the same
divine finger that burned the bush,

stripped sandals from my feet, pointed
me back to the teeth of the Nile.

We chose to live through years
of plagues; locusts climbing from

our mouths, the stink of holy cattle
rotting on the plains, years of waiting

at night for fire in the desert, forgetting
the blood smeared on our foreheads,

door sills, feeling alone—as all who live
in darkness feel lonely.

GOD OF DEW

Tell me how to taste
      that first rush of God
           like the high of a lightning
    bolt, to peer up at the sky
and know: the sky looks back.
      This thick book and only
           one story seems to matter
    today; it's morning, and before
Gideon turns, the wool could be wet
      and it could be dry. Schrödinger
           has nothing on this unturned
    sheep, like a hardcover book,
no cracks in its spine—yet.
      Tomorrow, whether damp or
           dry, you will tell me there is no
    God-of-dew, God-of-lamb pelt,
or unopened tome. Which sounds,
      to me, like tomb. Tell me
           the taste on the warrior's lips
    at dawn when he shook out
the skin and found an answer.

LEGEND

    After 'The Six Swans' by the Brothers Grimm

To break the curse, you cannot
speak. This choice defines you: mute,

fingers stinging nettles, your brothers
a wreath of white birds curled

around your sleeping form, flashes
of the boys they once were fading in and out

of dusk. Even at your wedding you hold
your tongue, make no promise—

after all, what vow can be wrung from
the dumb, which oath is stronger

than your silence? When he touches you
in a strange land, you don't say a word.

As your children are pried from your
bleeding hands, one after another, you cry

soundlessly. Babes, shirts, years, baskets
of thorny herbs, nothing you can count aloud.

When at last they light the pyre to burn you,
when at last you throw your weaving onto

blistering swans, when at last your brothers,
transformed, cut you free with blades red

as your fingers—what sound will come out,
if any? Is this the version where they slay

crowds to a man, your kin, keen as needles,
still blooming feathers? Where you scorch

your stepmother for stealing your young?
This, the woman's legend: thankless, painful,

written down by men—theirs the only word
worth anything.

MOUTHFUL OF ORCHIDS

You never wanted absolution: forgiveness is bitter

tincture on the lips, absinthe & arsenic. Instead:

have a mouthful of orchids. High cheekbones

powdered with lead. Better: a beast's body to hold

you in its teeth, heartbeat rabbiting

against hot tongue. Acid in a perfume bottle.

A snake's unhinging jaw, gulping heron's

open throat. Breath of noxious oxides, a list

of names forgotten, a matchbox soaked in sulfur.

Best: a bed wet with gasoline, a radioactive bathtub

to soak in until you glow.

CULLET

I've swallowed glass for every bottle
you drank. Call me terror. Call me
reckonings you looked for
in the bathroom mirror. Call

me *shit that oughta been slapped
out* when you were younger, before the old
men touched you in a stained
-glass cathedral. Call me window

broken by your ruined knuckles. My
blood is your blood; our past in silver
slivers on tile floors. Compared to you, I am
summer that never ends, tempered glass,

a nest of unhatched eggs. I say *hello* & you
pray my name back to me.

HAOLE GIRL

In class, a girl taps my shoulder—*where did you come from?*
I mean to say *origin does not equal belonging*, but when I open
my mouth, I taste humidity & rotting mangoes, salty limu,
metallic a'a rock after heavy rain. When I was young, coarse
hair rivering to my waist, I looked like a nearly-native tree.
Kind Aunty K sewed six fabric pa'u skirts for me with nimble
fingers, taught me kaholo, ha'a, uwehe, kaholo again. Her bare
feet were gorgeous & silent on the stone floor. Dry wind
from the Mauna, clouds gathered around its waist like a heavy
skirt. Trading a dollar at the market to a fierce woman for spam
musubi and a quarter, fingered & forgotten in my pocket
through the rainy season. The kupuna who taught me to bend
ti leaves into magic shapes, fish & lures, hats & leis. Playing
Kōnane at the park with my brother, bone coral white against
smooth pahoehoe. *You know King Kamehameha won with a single
move?* The stink of wild boar rotting at the edge of a dirt road.
The moana with many names like the vast skirt of the earth.
The crunch of opihi at a graduation party laden with leis, fireworks,
someone's father trading the cops beer not to notice.
The uncles clearing paths after hurricanes. The hurricanes on
my birthday every year like a present. The Mauna protecting us
from the storm. The protectors under Costco tarps on the Mauna.
The flag, battered, monarchy colors shining like parrot fish
on a line. The 'āina I grew on like an imported fruit, introduced
crop, invasive flock, nourished by rainwater, poi, malasadas.
'Āina I winged away from like a migratory bird—*I can never return.*

DOL 돌

At one hundred days old, my brother was laid out on a table.

My brother in silk hanboks, wrapped like a meal.

My brother, chubby and ruddy, thick fingers grasping, face round as a dinner plate.

    It was a ceremony for a firstborn son:
    Residue of a belief that we choose our own destiny
    as if fate can fit in a baby's fist.

    One hundred offerings were laid out on a table:
    Halmeoni herding him toward a worn Bible.
    Our father fluttering dollar bills like butterflies.
    Halabeoji stroking the long, wise line of a calligraphy brush.

Me, in our mother's arms, watching a choice I never had from across the room.

Though firstborn, I am no son.

Gumming at his fingers, unbothered, my brother pulled a red string:
slippery and bright, emblem of a long life.

    When he ran away in first grade, was rushed to the ER in college, slipped into sickness,
    I grasped for his string, praying for him to live *this long*.

We wait one hundred days for dol in case the child dies young.

    It was in his defense on a playground that I first flashed my teeth,
    growled at an older bully like an animal, my brother still and quiet behind me.
    No one can pick on him but me.

There was a time I wanted nothing more than to lift my brother myself.

> Our parents, worried at my small frame, his newborn body, buckled me into a baby carrier and sat us on the floor, so I could wrap my arms all the way around him—as if my tiny limbs were a shield against the outside world, and I alone could carry him.

A friend told me I said *brother* softer than any other word.

GALATEA AGAIN

i cannot love you the way
      you want; each time i
swallow the *no* you pull

      fingers through my hair,
thumb my ankle bone. i want
      the safety of a river rock,

quartzite smiles, to watch
      your lashes fold lapis
into iris, blue into green

      for years. your knuckles
were granite with small chips
      where my teeth sunk in.

i left pockets of silence
      like opals under your
cover within the ripples

      of your mattress, glove
compartment, even between
      your palms, like a prayer.

but you never had an ear
      for stones—can you hear
anything i'm not saying?

CRUEL INSTINCTS

The bird, gasping,
fills my palms with frantic warmth. I will
her to live. Her beak tips to the sky,
to the glass so clear, she almost
sailed through it. I already know
she will die. Metallic feathers blink
black-green on her working throat,
reminding me of the goat that tangled
in the barbed-wire fence, one stiff
hoof hooked at the wrong angle.
Reminding me of the look on your face—
its dear and painful hope, the savage sickle
of optimism. I tip glass-clear sugar
water into her mouth, breathe hot
air onto her belly. How many extra hours
have I forced her to stay? So you see,
one day, I will do it. The exact
worst thing. You, dragging
it out like a wounded animal,
and me, letting it live.

A STAR IS COLLAPSING IN CYGNUS

Small specks of light fold into themselves
by the swan in the sky, just a stellar neighborhood

away, while I commute the 75 through Seattle.
Between one breath and the next, it banks and

pinches out like a flame; a small black spot, gone
faster than the bird god took the girl, swallowed

her up, planting celestial seeds in the bruised
dark where it happened. And no matter how

many times my bus circles this block, my pencil
orbiting her name, I can't escape the burning

labor of a dying sun, the black hole pushing
through her legs to be born. Some violence

is so big, you can see it from space: supernova,
buckling into dark matter, bleeding bright dust

in rivers across the way. Some woundings
are witnessless: a girl crying, feathers in her hair—

FIRST HYMN

Heaven said: waters, split. Stars, open up
your mouths and scream. Animals, shed your skin

and be naked. Heaven said—behold, the blood
is paid, the crushed hand healed, the gouged

eye scooped back in the socket. The fruit remains
uneaten on the trees. Fields sweated into rivers,

dust settled, while angels blinked their thousand
wings, each feather a star, a pupil pointed in wonder

toward earth, the dim, celestial marble where the first
hymn ended. Rocks cried out. A child was born.

THALASSOPHOBIA

The absence of fear is a failure
of imagination.

Beneath the ocean's surface,
sirens lure with the promise of what's

known, never to reveal the twisting tail hidden
below. The terror of sharks pales once

you've heard the heartbeat of the planet's oldest
song, the blue press of an unbearably

vast embrace. Anything could lurk below;
not even sound echoes in the darkness

of some subaquatic trenches, not even
light. What secrets swell

in the deep. I've learned to inhabit my own
body. This arm only stretches so far, these fingers?

Mine. They close around the current and brine
escapes between knuckles. In the ocean, lines

blur, only skin separates my flesh
from the unknown. Water unfolds beyond

sight, its body stretches forever. This is the great
fear that yawns under the surface. Do you see it?

BURNING THE SHIPS

The return

will be painful. You will lose

more than you believed you were

blessed with, each glory, at loss, with interest.

You will survive, impossibly, carved from many memories—

Odysseus, snagged on islets, crew scattered, men devoured. A sea

salmon pulled inevitably up a clear, fresh stream. Oriental blossom on tropical

islands, orchid in the brine, suckling salt water. Song from a bird given up as extinct

for generations, heard, miraculously, once again. Endurance, like story, shared through mouths,

blood, fires. The offerings we burned and did not. The ashed ships on the beach left behind. The truth:

a hard, hot coal, bright on a distant shore. A lesson I learned later than the salmon, orchid, songbird: there is

no going back.

GLASS EEL

We call the unnameable beast that lives at the edge
of a map *leviathan*, ancient sea creature from the depths
of scripture. God knows every animal, but left their naming
to us, a parent closing the keys to the house in a child's
hands. Freshwater eels sometimes spawn in captivity,
but no one has found a single wild egg. Instead, young glass
larvae are scooped from the Pacific and raised for consumption.
It should be impossible to eat a question, a species with no
known origin and a sex life so mysterious, it slips
into myth. I have held myth inside my mouth:
unagi bowl slick with tare that soaked through the rice.
In the East, we say seven deities live in a single grain.
I remember the first time eucharist bread melted
on my tongue. You see what I am saying? We have eaten God,
you and I. We are each complicit in the communion of living.

FISH EYE

We fought over them after dinner, my brother
and I. Two salty beads, milk-white,

floating in a wrinkled silver face,
spine of exposed splinters, chili

oil blood on the table before us. Clear
green tea running into my mother's

tiny cup. What couldn't be eaten at that table?
Scars on Halmeoni's bare feet from

shrapnel are sour as kimchi.
Sorrow, drunk heartily from translucent

soju bottles. Each tragedy made small
as short-grained rice, anything we couldn't

swallow pried like fish ribs from my bleeding
gums. The present has a way of ballooning

until the future and past touch, warping
at the edges of my vision. This moment:

a fish-eye lens, broken eulogy, dark medicine,
lunch. The world outside, bland as water

juk, noses wrinkling at our smell.
Within, a plate turned toward me,

chopsticks pressed against my lips. My ancestors
asking, 여우 새끼, aren't you hungry?

GRETEL & HANSEL WHEN ASKED WHY THEY ARE HUNGRY

But we have never been full. Mother,
dying, left us empty, milk

dregs sloshed in our lonely
stomachs, father's love like bread

crumbs during Lenten fasting.
Our lives a fasting with no end,

no season of reprieve. Starved,
we sucked on stones, watched

the strange woman in our home,
unblinking. And what would you

have done, hands full of honey,
fists of crumbled ginger mortar,

smashed panes of sugar glass?
Have you ever been in this pain?

When the oven flickered, we saw
it was hungry, too. For us or her,

it did not matter. And who are we
to deprive the beast? Hot metal

animal, licking fiery lips. Here,
eat your dinner.

MY GRANDMOTHER AFTER KOREA

gained three more tongues and never learned
to bite any of them. Fierce and only 4'11", we rarely saw
eye to eye. She told me stories, laughing as she scoured
me with soapy water: the dry fluff of popcorn kernels,
nearly too hot to touch, sold at market to pay
for school. How she ate each of them, one after another.
She raised piglets to escape her father's second wife,
carefully rotating them so the littlest had enough to eat.
Words she did not have to say: after the war,
there was never enough food. How Japanese names
clung to her family long after the annexation ended,
no matter how hard she scrubbed. How of course
it was a restaurant she opened in the new country,
although people said she ate dogs instead of ducks.
How, when she was stripped of her old name
and told she should choose a new, easier one,
she didn't even hesitate to say: *Joy*.

LATCHING

When I was born, I did not feed
for three days. My mother's nipples swollen
with mastitis, too thick to latch onto
or swallow around, the nurse hissing *the worst case
I've ever seen* as she milked mom's breasts
on the living room floor. I cried,
ravenous. How did I know to be hungry?

I heard a kitten weaned
too early will keep suckling her whole
life, mouth searching blankets, elbows, strangers,
for what she needs. My condition was not caused
by the lack of milk, but its abundance. Bud
too rich to latch. Drink too rich to taste. This,
an ancient contradiction: to be surrounded by plenty,
and still starve.

THE WOLF, REMEMBERED

Wet fur, teeth, pawprints linger
in my dreams, the forest with its soft sighs

remembers and I think: my skin cannot be
my skin; it cannot be torn from the body

which swallowed my body, and so
I do not want it. These bloody hands

are mine—they wash the hide of who
I was, and although he

is dead, damp breath forever faded
from the earth, his yellow eyes watch

my steps, pause at the buried axe,
my grandmother's grave still turned

with loamy earth. Perhaps in another life
I would be the wolf and haunt his trails,

looming in the shadows, loose jowls
tasting his cloak.

VAMPIRE PLANTS TALK TO THEIR VICTIMS WHILE DRINKING

Lately I've been moved
by how quickly you lean

into my touch, fear
in the past. I now understand

the horned *oni* king, cradling
his human wife, three eyes

blinking in exquisite dilemma:
whether he loves her

too much to eat her, or enough.
Patience and adoration the required

ingredients in aged wine: young
wives, rich liquid swirls

within cups and cheeks, lips
and bottles, viscous, viscus.

The vines of the vampire
plant swell around words

we don't say: parasite, addiction,
sister witchweed, cousin

broomrape, limbs tangled
around crops, lawns, bodies,

gentle susurrus since a host
tastes better if you talk to it

as it dies—I'm here for you,
I feel your pain. There is a waxing

for every waning. First,
I lose sleep and peace, then comes

the pallor. I don't pull away.
Around us is a constant

cadence, an ancient clinging,
almost a song—I could live

without you, but why?

TURTLE SHIP

My father loved to tell me about the first iron ship, the geobukseon (거북선) or "turtle ship," which was instrumental military technology in Korea's Joseon era. The ship defended the Korean peninsula from invasion for nearly 400 years. In the 1980s, my father's family emigrated from Seoul to the United States.

We left our home
and we never looked
back, though the wind
spat in our faces
and the tides below the boats
begged us to turn
around, fatherland
fading into blue
mountains, vanished
persimmon trees, our
grandparents' still & mighty
graves. We watched great
serpents strangle the waters, bit
into raw sea cucumbers.
We buried our names
at sea, baptized our tongues
in the salt of a new
horizon, blistered
fingers on sunned
wood and ropes severed
from our birthplace.
Hope sailed with us,
the turtle shell shielding
our backs, hope, the chop
stick we poked into turtle

brains to bleed them
for soup during war. Hope,
another kind of meal
we drank day after day,
aubade of bitter iron
& brine. Hope: the lifejackets
lost to storms, hope, the ship
vomiting us into a foreign
state. Hope the iron shoes we built
out of its body, and hope,
our home, old
& new, the land
that devoured us.

DANJI GIRL

Wait for persimmons to ripen on the trees, for eggs to hatch,
leaves to wither. You rip fistfuls of rooster feathers from

flesh, wash rice, mend the pig pen, again, bury kimchi
in the garden for the winter. One day, soldiers will tear through

the fences, spill the rice, steal the meat; your father will hide
under floorboards where the ondol fires warm you through long

winters. The floods will come, bridges bombed from here to
Busan. Pale GIs camp two nights by the village in their thick

-soled boots, their hair the color of bones. They will split cans
for your budae jjigae while you dig for pickle jars under frost.

Decades pass; police will beat old men in town square, so you
bundle your children onto old boats, steam across the sea, plant

roots in flat lands far from your grandfathers' graves, the mountain
range, persimmon trees. Someday you will give yourself a new

name, watch grandchildren grow with no memory of your home,
while you still grind peppers and raise cabbage, salt brine,

spread paste, fill heavy earthenware pots with your fire.

PHAEDRA

Would it ease the ache, to hold
a man between your legs?
Would it break the curse, to wed
the father, then his son?
You rise in fever, weep in silence,
carve words without witness.
Can you keep the secret? You made
the accusation, sentence; you
execute—and after you have dug
the grave, filled, and buried it,
will you regret you were not loved, or
did not love enough? You,
whose name means light, who lives
in darkness too deep to see.

LIGHT A CANDLE

Be a prophet, said no one, ever. Be in pain, and either
blind or mad because nothing comes free. Be alone,
and have no one believe you. Sleep badly while the glow
from your eyes illuminates dirty bedroom walls. Be there before it
ever happens and still be too late. What kind of sick curse
becomes destiny, no line between character and fate,
each push to life pushed back from an equal and opposite
direction? Beware: when each day your two cupped beggar
palms try to gather light like water and catch nothing. Be
afraid of the things that move within you. Belladonna night
consumes you, thick with creatures—eyeless and dreaming.
Be careful not to know too much before they cut out your
tongue, curse your words to wander like flightless birds.
Truth beckons, bewitching and slick. Do not believe.
The future will call, like gold-warm fleece, dawning sun,
like one candle in the yawning dark. Look away.

CLAUSTROPHOBIA

The air is thick, the tunnel
not thick enough. Where
have you gone? The ceiling
is low, the sky sinking into
the yellow glare of a lone
flashlight. You laugh and offer
it to me. We crawl, hands
and knees scraping wet stone,
cold moss. I hate the air
in my lungs, I hate the light
at my back. Endless pressure—
as if we were once again inside
our mother. You thought this
would be fun, swallowed
by the lava tube's vast throat.
Squeezed through veins in
the earth like its blood. Mist
on my skin turns to sweat,
the cave breathes, small
brave plants burrow even to
this depth. Our path dips
down, then curves up
an organ. I look for you
in darkness, my eyes holes.
Is it worse to be alone
or not alone? My fingers
bleed. I've forgotten
to breathe. The tunnel dilates
and shudders. If we survive
this, I will kill you. If we
survive this, I will be born anew.

I WANT TO WANT TO GET BETTER

They tell me depression is an upside down
house of mirrors, everything
reflected in the wrong direction, from every
direction. I say: I am starting to see
in photographic negative. Black eyes with
bleached pupils, irises like collapsing
stars. They say, have some tea. Live
in the moment. But how
can you let yourself be held by the stiff hands
of a clock when they tick endlessly
backward? Why would I drink tea when
everything is seen through the bleak stare
of a camera shutter? History cuts like silver
shards on the bathroom floor. The future
reaching; skeletal flower stems touch
white shadows on my wall. I can't
get out of bed. Instead, I stare at drapes like silent
wraiths. They shield me from the forgotten sun,
painful to see, lens overexposed,
each star, a gaping wound in my darkness.

EPISTLE OF EVE

I'm not sorry for the fruit.
Instead, forgive me for the rib
wasted on my muddied flesh.
I'll never know how much you bled
in that grassy sleep or, upon
waking, how loud your long
and wordless scream. Forgive
me for the snake who always seems
to follow in his twining way, scales
flecked with dusk, eyes smooth
and lidless. I couldn't see
the lie. You know I'd accept sunken
teeth again and again to undo
that one. More sorry for the children
we buried together—twins devoured
in my womb, Abel engulfed
by his own wheaten field, daughters
scattered, like ashes, over many waters.
Sorry for the times our feet bled
on the dusty road, for the flaming sword
seared into every dream. I'm sorry
to have learned shame, and known
myself to be naked, heard
and lost the great voice in the garden,
watched our sons sink
past the sun-brushed horizon
until my eyes stung in the light of it.
But my love, I'm not sorry
for the fruit. Husband,
you ate it, too.

HAOLE SONNET

I learned thousands of these little knowings:
how to pluck bold rooster feathers, steam ti
leaves, bury pork shank under an imu's
coals for two days until tender, always
they were patient with me, although I am
unteachable. Years of small wisdoms: here
this, how that, and when to finger-comb black
beaches for peridot, pluck ripe ruby
guava, find fresh fish by their clear, glassy
eyes, and still, I hardly know my name, and
how to swim, and where to pray. Small gods lived
inside the breadfruit trees and snow-capped peaks
but I have closed my shell to their voices.
Kupuna, where have they buried your name?

THE MILKY WAY DREAMS OF THE BIG BANG

I'm counting losses. Solar systems crushed between teeth, the spiraling embrace
of whole galaxies. How many stars were devoured by the black hole garbage disposal?

We used to be closer together. Brilliance held captive in one
bright point, like birds in the same house. Then radiance decayed. The universe flowered,

expanding. We fucked each other, waged war, milky blood spilled across the sky.
Perhaps there was never peace, only our own unshakable nostalgia. I knew

the suns by name, their brilliance, their genders. Then they were renamed
& renamed & renamed. We are all constellating farther apart. I have nothing

to offer you in this inflatable universe. Except always. Except if I can recall
the holy command that broke me into being. Except maybe it was actually

a question, words ever reverberating, half-remembered, in a mouth offered & beloved.

DNA TEST

Follow the spit all the way back to your ancestors.
      The past is a deep pool and I'm drowning
to find the stories that seeped between the cracks

      of generations, match names to the disappeared.
Drag cotton swab inside your cheek, the test instructs.
      I mail it in a plastic vial: a message in a bottle.

Blood tells the truth long after the records
      have been burned. The papers lost in war: birth certificates,
marriage licenses, documents in a hybrid language

      only Halabeoji can read. I drove 200 miles to steal back
the photographs on my kitchen wall, shelled out $50
      to untangle my DNA. I pretend a lab can answer

the questions that haunt my introductions—*where
      are you from?* or *do you feel more Korean or American?*
I peer closely at my results like a palm reading, as if this sheet

      of paper could tell me who was raped in the annexation,
killed in refugee camps, any more than it knows the love
      stories strong enough to elope across the ocean, birth

ten children, survive starvation. What can saliva archive?
      Does it know which great-great-grandfather swung which
sword? How grandmother's grandmother rode horseback

      from Michigan to Arkansas, seven months pregnant, sick
of the cold. Of course not: veins are not paths, my open palms
      are not a map, and there is no test to gauge the living.

BACKWARDS

I want to never see that look
on your face again. No, I want

never to have seen it at all. As if
a broken bone couldn't only heal, but *unbreak*.

As if the setting sun could be sucked
out of the sea to rise in the west.

You were always so patient with me. If that
were something that could be deserved,

I wouldn't deserve it. I bite my tongue
until a callus forms, thick and lumpy

like rhino hide, but the words have long
escaped. I wish for the nonsense

of Superman, whizzing around the world
backwards to rewind time like a VHS tape.

In real life, Lois wouldn't make it. You said
you regretted nothing, but were sorry

for making me cry. That look on your face
flickered like a screen, your eyes liquid.

Understanding had sunk into you, a stone
dropped into a deep lake where the light

doesn't touch. I've only regretted two things, really,
my whole life. But God, do I regret them.

FIRELINE

My grandfather burned
fields as a boy, starving
wildfires before they tore

into the village. His face,
smoke-smudged, glows
at me in sepia. He knew

fire & witness is another
flame. After his mother
died, he ashed her photographs,

paper wings fluttering
in a cigar box & now he can't
remember her likeness. I wish

I could have told him
not all reckonings are soot—
the torched city soldiers

crunched through, snowmelt
on scorched crops. I'd say
we are also known by living

things, thinking of the tree
a crashed bike grew into, seeds
nourished by flash fires,

smooth, righteous nuts
shining through soil. Thinking
of family he planted in a foreign land,

wild bouquets we picked
for him as children, fingers raw
with pollen. Willowherb, fire

poppy, pheasant's eye:
because of his smile, we never
thought of them as weeds.

ORIGIN OF SPECIES

Let the strongest live
and the weakest die
you said, spinning a beer
bottle cap with opposable

thumbs. As your words
echoed, I thought of my friend
admitted to emergency
with water in her lungs

and eyes—or my mother,
bedridden in those early
years, hands gentle in my
hair, though her body

tore at her body day after
day. The unrelenting
tenderness she offered
failing orchids, nursing

them into health she
couldn't have. I remain
skeptical that ten thousand
years of Darwin's

history amounts to this:
your bald cruelty, flat, un
-seeing gaze, receding
hairline. I've lived here

so long, the myth
has become truth: as if
*the preservation of favored
races* is all that matters

in the struggle for life.
I wonder what look
would have flowered on
Charles's face at your blunt

application of his words,
how carefully his fingers
brushed the soft flesh
of prized star orchids

in the quiet ecosystem
of his greenhouse.
My mother called
yesterday—is it evolution

that makes her voice so
beautiful to me? Have I
inherited mercy as a trait
of failed natural selection,

like my poor lungs and feeble
eyes? Go on, drink beer, quote
the dead, my vestigial creed
is evolving as we speak:

let the weakest survive
and live gloriously. May
every fragile blossom
exhale our victory.

OPHIDIOPHOBIA

    great grandmother barefoot   daily crossed the river   thick with water

moccasins cotton   mouths their open jaws   like white-fleshed flowers

     her fear   distilled across generations   grandmother couldn't bear

to hear the word   *snake*   fingernails digging   into my arm

     is that an s-word   we had to hide   their twisted images

dishtowels thrown   over nat geo covers   gold-scaled bracelets

     concealed under sleeves   zoo pamphlets tucked   in the back of the bin

but not for my mother   her garden gloves   perfumed with earth

     pointing out a garter or ribbon   sluicing through grass

saying *save your fear*   *for when you need it*   and so i learned to find

     shining eyes and quick tongues sweet   generations laugh at their puzzled faces

and one day   at a library exhibit   i was the only one to hold her

     vast goldenrod python   muscling over my shoulders   the teacher explained

her lineage   i didn't listen   palms smoothing down   soft buttercup scales

LUCID FEVER

Lung-scarred, rattle
-breathed, a waif, I will always
fear drowning on land,

abandoned by the wind
gods, kami kaze 神風, *breath
of the sky*. You spooned

medicine: black herbs,
elderberry, valerian,
painted frankincense

and tea tree perfume in
holy pockets at my wrists,
hollows of my throat. When

undertows snapped at
my ankles, you
rescued me. I still taste

seaspit vomit on the sand,
salt and kelp, a backwards
inhalation.

In the absence of breath,
the heart squeezes tight.
If I wear this halo,

I trust you to unbury me.

PORTRAIT OF THE FRIGHTENED IN RECOVERY

you see,
i'm unlearning
the world all the time.
anxieties picked apart like
embroidery stitches. of course,
as a child, i feared nothing. my mother
was there. i dashed about with the urgency
of an endangered animal, devoured ants and clover,
scaled trees, scowled at strangers, returned, always, to the quiet
shade of my mother's paint-stained apron, her gentle quietness that never felt
like silence. every child believes their mother is magic, but now i know it to be true. how
many nights did i call, palms slipping against phone case, to say *you were right?*
the lack of judgment on the other side of the line. years before
claustrophobia crushed the air from my lungs, i wanted
my mother to squeeze me back into her body.
i felt safe when we touched. my brother
and i pressed into her as she read
fairytales in the light of a cheap,
paper lamp, three of us
becoming one same,
safe creature in
its glow.

GOD'S LOVE IS VERY LOUD

Though I can hardly hear
over the river
draining out of Eden like a bath
tub, the heady
rushing of the day. I am very busy
being in pain,
and the bottle is so far away.
Demons live
in seven of my teeth and the others
need whitening.
My husband is always asleep. I don't even
like fruit. How
can he hear anything? Maybe it's
tinnitus. Too
many Percocets. The children
need picking
up from school; the orchard
is overripe.
We must have been happy, once,
but the perfect
love they imagine is an animal
you never
named. The dishes need doing: I
scrub & scrub
but zest lingers beneath my nails.

CITRUS PARADISI

In Chicago, the sunny kitchen smelled like grapefruit, wood dust, wool coats. The windy, wide paved streets felt empty, even when they were full. The oro blanco grapefruit tasted richest in the coldest months, separated into perfect, jewel-toned triangles. Did you know some people on depression medication can't eat grapefruit? Not even the LaCroix flavor. Not even ruby reds, head-sized grapefruits that glisten at Trader Joe's, only 30 cents above my budget! Juicy, smelling like morning, smelling like the January I almost killed myself, but didn't. We split them in halves—sour, and sometimes so, so sweet—redblush grapefruit in blue china bowls, we ate them on the icy roof with toothy steel spoons. They say there are as many kinds of friendship as fruit, or cars, like your old truck, its rumble rumble over road salt, crisp ice, back from the grocery store, the compostable green baggy bursting open and out rolled grapefruit! So many huge, fleshy pink grapefruits; when they toppled to the ground, they bounced. I ate one this morning, thumbs dug deeply in thick skin, glad to be alive, and every time I eat one, I think of you.

IN HAWAIIAN, HAOLE MEANS BREATHLESS

Outsider. As in, when you clasp
hands and breathe each
other's spirit, there is no
spirit to breathe. My lungs

are weak. A lesson I learned
young. A Kona shore spat
me out, vomiting brine, sand
in my ears and eyes. *The land*

can reject you or keep you
safe a local man told me, his skin
leather, patting my back
as I puked. *I broke my collar*

bone on the beach right
there, he said, pointing at the perfect
surf. The *ha* in *haole* and *aloha*
means breath. *Aloha,* the most

beautiful word I know. Like *aroha,*
the Māori word for *pity* and *love.* The long
exhale. The way you say it when
you come. And when you go.

THE POET'S GUIDE TO TRANSLATION

Question everything: the creak
of the bridge and the crook
of the stair; be wary of the dry,
knocking trees, the ochre in
your daughter's eyes—trust
nothing to be only what you ask
of it. Cherry blossoms
blushing in spring don't know
your story; glass eels slip
through tidal pools, nearly
invisible. They do not exist
only for your eyes. Watch snow
thicken and let yourself
be cold—then at last we will speak
the same language; the image
will open herself to you, and leaves
will still be leaves in translation.

CATCHING

I'm eight with a matchbox in my pocket.
I only know a few things: squirrels

don't hibernate in Michigan; librarians
don't vote for Bush. Snow melts

on my lashes, my hand-me-down jacket,
but I linger by the chain-link, wise enough

to anticipate another round of standardized
tests and too small to avoid them.

I thumb one matchstick, pinches of sulfur.
Someone said *No Child Left Behind*. A teacher

is coming to get me. I was born into a long
line of flame-mongers: my father spinning

cans of coals over a bone-dry field, his
father feeding flames with Japanese books,

photographs of his dead mother. They find me
too late, tinder already buried beneath a tree,

no evidence in my pockets, backpack, locker.
I asked my father why he did it—his regret

was palpable after the crop caught ablaze. He said
I don't know or I was a fool and once, face lit

by a tame campfire, *you should have seen it—
when the sparks flew fast they were so beautiful.*

YA'ABURNEE

After we dug up
 the pit & buried
  her beside the boar

skull, crushed cat, one
 of the hens & five
  strangled roosters

there was no more
 room for dying.
  You have to live

I told the breathing
 animals: seed-eyed chicks
  with down soft as sunlight,

jewel-bright flashes
 of betta fish, my black
  cat. We spent years

not talking about
 my cat dying & I won't
  start now. Cemeteries

hold twelve or so
 hundred bodies per
  acre, heavy as a ship

berth, each body
    shrouded in velvet
        on beds of cement.

The wet earth keeps
    its secrets: crops,
        seeds, bones, promises

& here's another—
    I love you too much
        to bury you.

MIRACLE

My mother said every seed that sprouts
is an act of mercy. I'm learning
to keep my ear to the earth. The more
angry I am, the more tenderly I plant
words on the page. Each letter clear,
deep enough to root. I do not know
if everyone deserves forgiveness,
but maybe it's true. I've spent
a lot of time preparing for its unbearable
heaviness, like Atlas rehearsing
in a weightlifting gym. Some days
are easier than others. And you see,
the other week I caught my father
in the garden, laying mulch
for my mother, looking at a flower
as if seeing it for the first time.
Mark says Christ healed a man born
blind, but not how painful it must
have been to see your whole life
stretch in front of you, and lost
and behind. I've tried to write this
poem twice already. If you can't hear
what I'm saying, I can't show you.

LAZARUS

I eat it to feel alive, a man confessed to me,
teeth crunching through a golden reaper so hot,
my eyes watered to be near. When did he feel alive?
Lazarus, I mean, after he died and then came back
again. We talk about him like a firebird, crumbling
to ash and shaking off the coals to rise once more.
But it must have been something, you know? Waking
from four days of death, frankincense cloying
the air, linen bandages unraveling. Did it feel good,
like stretching after a days-long nap or did it sting
like capsaicin, dormant limbs burning from lack
of use? My father once ate a ghost pepper whole.
First came the sweat, then vomiting. *I think
I'm dying,* he told me, *my life is flashing by my eyes*.
And that's another question—what did he see,
between? The glow of seven stars in a pierced
right hand, a double-edged sword emerging
from his mouth—perhaps the world tilted
in resurrection like from a devastating concussion,
swirling around his sisters' grief-creased faces.
Sometimes I leap from cliffs, cling to bridges,
swim with sharks, but I'm not brave enough to suck
a devil's tongue, weep into a pile of sliced scotch
bonnets, try to grill another chocolate habanero.
Maybe the question I most wish I could ask
Lazarus is which hurt more—the fever that burned
him to death from the inside, or the rush of God,
like a Trinidad Scorpion, like ten million Scoville
shocking him alive to the face of a friend?

OMPHALOPHOBIA

In yoga class, I press my stomach to the mat,
    an instructor urging me to *find*

your center while I recall the girl who cried
    when I tucked a knuckle all the way

inside my belly button, gut swallowing
    the tip. My finger probed, as if

I could feel the organs underneath. Some
    people fear knot-like navels

can unravel, intestines unspooling. Such
    a secret place, a whole world

populated by bacteria—an early mouth, tether
    to where you came from. In many

places, umbilical remnants are kept sacred,
    the last tie to parents, ancestors,

home. I move through the asana; my middle
    tightens, belly button flickering

like an eye at a keyhole. The meditative practice
    of navel-gazing, *omphaloskepsis*,

was said to bring calm, grounding, celestial
    joys. I breathe harshly, my practice

done. *Treat yourselves tenderly*, the teacher
    says. I wipe sweat from my brow,

smooth one palm down my torso to cup my navel,
    as if anyone could protect the origin of a scar.

ORIGIN OF THE FEAR

We have such beautiful names
for terrible things:

lightning, pelagic, extinguish, every phobia
I could hope to catalog.

And all of them
are just your body

speaking in the voice
of an ancient ancestor—

survive, she says. Though your hands shake
and your stomach

bruises. Survive, as static crawls
up the inside of your skull and gun

shots punctuate your street's
silence. Every fear opens

its ugly mouth only to speak in her soft,
familiar voice, sing the song

of every mother
like the darkest lullaby, her body

curled around a crying
baby, holding the darkness out

with her own shape.
Survival the one, best song she knows,

stitching the centuries together note
by note.

Notes

The epigraph quotes the late Andrea Gibson's poem "I Sing the Body Electric, Especially When My Power's Out."

"Origin Myth" references "How many centuries deep is your wound?" which can be attributed to the Arabic poet Adonis from his book *If Only the Sea Could Sleep*.

"Phantom Pain as Natal Philopatry" refers to natal philopatry or natal homing, which is an animal's instinct to return to their birthplace.

The hangul script in "My Father after Korea" reads 그는 어디 있니? and translates to "*where is he?*"

"Second Tongue" includes the hangul 아라야 that translates to "arah-ya" which is the author's name with an affectionate honorific, commonly used for children.

"Her Name was Daphne" refers to the Greek myth of the nymph Daphne, daughter of Peneus, who escaped Apollo's insatiable lust by becoming a laurel tree. Afterwards, Apollo took the laurel as one of his special symbols.

"God of Dew" interacts with the story of Gideon and the wool from Judges 6:36-40. It also refers to the "Schrödinger's Cat" thought experiment.

"Haole Girl" references numerous examples of ʻŌlelo Hawaiʻi, or Native Hawaiian language. "Paʻu" refers to a fabric skirt used in hula dance and "*kaholo, haʻa, uwehe*" are traditional dance steps. Kōnane is an ancient Hawaiian strategy board game using white and black stones that works similarly to the game "Leap Frog." Because of this, it is impossible to win in very few moves, but King Kamehameha, who was known to favor the game, was rumored to have impossibly won in a single maneuver. "The protectors under Costco tarps on the Mauna" refers to the Mauna Kea protests against construction of the Thirty Meter Telescope on the holy mountain which resulted in ongoing demonstrations from 2014 to 2020 spearheaded by Native Hawai'i residents.

"Dol 돌" is short for doljanchi, the traditional Korean "first" birthday celebration.

"Galatea Again" refers to the Greek myth of Pygmalion who carved an idealized woman out of ivory and fell in love with it.

"Fish Eye" uses the hangul "여우 새끼" which translates to "yeou saekki" which means fox cub.

"Out of the Eater" contains numerous references to the Biblical narrative of Samson and Delilah from Judges 16.

"The Wolf, Remembered" references some older versions of the Brothers Grimm folktale "Little Red Riding Hood" or ATU 333.

"Kumiho 구미호" refers to an East Asian mythological fox creature, often with nine tails, which takes the form of a beautiful woman to consume livers and hearts and/or seduce men. She is the result of patriarchal Confucian tradition and often the scapegoat for infidelity or even rape. The "yeowoo guseul" is a kind of magical pearl or marble the can be used to absorb energy and is often transferred by mouth via a kiss.

"Vampire Plants Talk to Their Victims While Drinking" references the parasitic plant *Cuscuta pentagona,* also known as strangleweed, which has been found to exchange mRNA communication with its host plants in recent studies (Tanya Lewis). Also mentioned in this poem are "oni," a kind of East Asian cryptid *yōkai*, similar to a demon, orc, ogre, or troll, particularly in Japanese folklore. While varying in appearance, oni often possess a third eye and/or extra digits and often consume humans. The particular oni referenced here can be traced to the animated series "Kakuriyo: Bed and Breakfast for the Spirits."

"A Star is Collapsing in Cygnus" refers to the Greek myth "Leda and the Swan" in which Zeus transforms into a swan to rape the queen of Sparta. Leda later gives birth to Castor, Pollux, Helen of Troy, and Clytemnestra. The constellation of Cygnus is named after this myth.

"Legend" refers to the Brothers Grimm fairytale "The Six Swans," or ATU 451. In this tale, an evil stepmother transforms the six sons of her husband's first marriage into swans. Their human sister endeavors to break the curse by making six shirts out of star flowers or nettles while not speaking for six years. In the fourth year, a king falls in love with the sister and marries her, producing two children but his mother steals the newborns and accuses the sister of having eaten them. When she finally breaks the curse, the youngest brother's shirt is often either incomplete or nonexistent, leaving him cursed. Sometimes the mother-in-law is then burned for accusing the sister.

"Danji Girl" references Korean traditional earthenware "danji" vessels, which could be buried to preserve pickled food, and budae jjigae, which is a World War II and Korean War dish derived from U.S. military food and Korean cuisine hybrids.

"Phaedra" refers to the Greek myth of the wife of Theseus, who fell in love with her stepson and was rejected. Afterward, she accused her stepson of rape, causing his death, and then killing herself.

"As If It Never Happened" refers to the Old Testament book of Exodus.

"Epistle of Eve" refers to stories from Genesis 2-4.

"Haole Sonnet" makes references to ʻŌlelo Hawaiʻi in the words "imu" or pitfire, and "kupuna" or elder.

"Origin of Species" quotes Charles Darwin's theory of evolution.

"Lucid Fever" references the kanji "神風" or "kamikaze" which means both "divine/godly wind" and the suicidal military branch of the Japanese army in World War II.

"God's Love is Very Loud" was inspired by a chapbook title by David Seung: "God's Love is Very Busy" (2019) published in Cathexis Northwest Press and references both Eve from Genesis 2 and the "seven devils" of Mary Magdalene in Luke 8:2 (KJV): "and certain women who had been healed of evil spirits and infirmities: Mary called Magdalene, out of whom went seven devils."

"Ya'aburnee" is an Arabic term which roughly translates to "you bury me" and expresses the desire to die before a loved one to never suffer their absence.

"Lazarus" engages with multiple elements from the story of Lazarus's death and resurrection in John 11. Numerous varieties of real peppers are also referenced: ghost pepper, scotch bonnet, devil's tongue, chocolate habanero, and Trinidad scorpion.

"Omphalophobia" references navel gazing meditation known as *omphaloskepsis* which is prevalent in Hinduism as well as certain Eastern Orthodox religious practices.

ACKNOWLEDGMENTS

Many thanks to the journals in which these poems first appeared, sometimes in different forms:

The American Poetry Review—"Astraphobia" & "Omphalophobia"
Colorado Review—"Cruel Instincts"
The Cresset—"As If It Never Happened" & "First Hymn"
diode—"Turtle Ship"
Frontier Poetry—"Catching"
Fugue—"God's Love is Very Loud"
Grimoire—"Her Name Was Daphne"
Grist—"My Grandmother After Korea"
Hyphen: Asian American Unabridged—"Fireline"
Lantern Review—"Kumiho 구미호"
Los Angeles Review—"The Poet's Guide to Translation"
Margins—"Vampire Plants Talk to Their Victims While Drinking"
New Ohio Review—"Lazarus"
New Reader Magazine—"I Want to Want to Get Better" & "Phaedra"
Ninth Letter—"Second Tongue"
Nimrod—"Origin of the Fear"
OnlyPoems—"Latching" & "Thalassophobia"
Pacifica Literary Review—"Sinter"
Palette Poetry—"Origin Myth"
Poets.org—"Haole Girl"
Relief—"Miracle"
RHINO—"Ophidiophobia"
River Styx—"Claustrophobia"
Ruminate—"Fish Eye" & "Eve Begun"
Rust+Moth—"God of Dew"
Salt Hill—"Phantom Pain as Natal Philopatry"
Sugar House Review—"Telephobia" & "Cullet"

Sidereal Magazine—"Haole Sonnet"
SIREN—"My Father After Korea," "The Wolf, Remembered," & "A Star is Collapsing in Cygnus"
The Threepenny Review—"Light a Candle"
Waxwing—"Glister" & "Out of the Eater"
the winnow—"Epistle of Eve"

This book would not be possible without the loving support of my family and poetry community:

My thanks to the MFA program at Ohio State University and the creative writing program at Wheaton College with special gratitude, respect, and appreciation for my teachers: Kathy Fagan, Marcus Jackson, and Miho Nonaka.

With love and heartfelt thanks to my workshop family who are a constant inspiration and without whom this collection would not have been born: Amanda Scharf, Eros Livieratos, Polley Poer, and Hannah Smith.

Gratitude to many discerning eyes who read these poems, including Marti Eads, David Seung, Lou Nelson, and Sarah Taylor Ko.

So many thanks to the editors and publishers who shared my work with the world.

For believing in *Brine Orchid* and for your insight, care, and attention, infinite thank yous to the mighty team at YesYes Books: KMA Sullivan and Gale Thompson.

Thank you to my grandparents and 조부모 for sharing your stories. For Elijah. But most of all for my parents who kept these tales alive—this one is for you.

A poet, editor, teacher, and fiction writer, Arah Ko is the author of *BRINE ORCHID* (YesYes Books 2025) and the chapbook *ANIMAL LOGIC* (Bull City Press 2026). Her work has been published or is forthcoming in *The American Poetry Review, Ninth Letter, RHINO, Colorado Review, The Threepenny Review, Quarterly West, Waxwing*, and elsewhere. She was awarded an Academy of American Poets Arthur Rense Prize, a Helen Earnhart Harley Creative Writing Fellowship Award in Poetry, and the 2021 Janet B. McCabe Poetry Prize. Arah hails from Hawai'i. She received her MFA in creative writing from the Ohio State University in Columbus where she served on the staff of *The Journal*. She is currently a Ph.D. student at The University of Cincinnati where she also serves on the staff of *The Cincinnati Review*.

Also by YesYes Books

FICTION
The Nothing by Lauren Davis
Girls Like Me by Nina Packebush
Three Queerdos and a Baby by Nina Packebush
Book of Exemplary Women by Diana Xin

WRITING RESOURCES
Gathering Voices: Creating a Community-Based Poetry Workshop by Marty McConnell

FULL-LENGTH POETRY COLLECTIONS
Ugly Music by Diannely Antigua
Bone Language by Jamaica Baldwin
Cataloguing Pain by Allison Blevins
Strange Flowers by Bryan Byrdlong
What Runs Over by Kayleb Rae Candrilli
Don't Cut Your Own Bangs by Caroline Crew
This, Sisyphus by Brandon Courtney
Salt Body Shimmer by Aricka Foreman
Gutter by Lauren Brazeal Garza
Forever War by Kate Gaskin
Inconsolable Objects by Nancy Miller Gomez
Ceremony of Sand by Rodney Gomez
Undoll by Tanya Grae
Loudest When Startled by luna rey hall
Everything Breaking / For Good by Matt Hart
Brine Orchid by Arah Ko
40 WEEKS by Julia Kolchinsky
murmurations by Anthony Thomas Lombardi
Sons of Achilles by Nabila Lovelace

Refusenik by Lynn Melnick
GOOD MORNING AMERICA I AM HUNGRY AND ON FIRE by jamie mortara
Born Backwards by Tanya Olson
a falling knife has no handle by Emily O'Neill
To Love an Island by Ana Portnoy Brimmer
Another Way to Split Water by Alycia Pirmohamed
Tell This to the Universe by Katie Prince
One God at a Time by Meghan Privitello
I'm So Fine: A List of Famous Men & What I Had On by Khadijah Queen
If the Future Is a Fetish by Sarah Sgro
Gilt by Raena Shirali
[insert] boy by Danez Smith
Say It Hurts by Lisa Summe
Hand Over Hand Over the Edge of the World by Patrick Swaney
Boat Burned by Kelly Grace Thomas
Helen Or My Hunger by Gale Marie Thompson
As She Appears by Shelley Wong

RECENT CHAPBOOK COLLECTIONS
Vinyl 45s
carried / in our own language by Tatiana Dolgushina
Exit Pastoral by Aidan Forster
Crown for the Girl Inside by Lisa Low
Phantasmagossip by Sara Mae
Year of the Sheep by Stacey Park
Scavenger by Jessica Lynn Suchon
Unmonstrous by John Allen Taylor
Giantess by Emily Vizzo

Blue Note Editions
Kissing Caskets by Mahogany L. Browne
One Above One Below: Positions & Lamentations by Gala Mukomolova
The Porch (As Sanctuary) by Jae Nichelle

www.ingramcontent.com/pod-product-compliance
Lightning Source LLC
Chambersburg PA
CBHW080454170426
43196CB00016B/2808